CONTE

CHOICE

Kwame Dawes • *Sturge Town* • Peepal Tree Press

RECOMMENDATIONS

Billy Collins • *Musical Tables* • Picador
Jasmine Cooray • *Inheritance* • Bad Betty Press
Kostya Tsolakis • *Greekling* • Nine Arches Press
David Wheatley • *Child Ballad* • Carcanet Press

SPECIAL COMMENDATION

Marjorie Lotfi • *The Wrong Person to Ask* • Bloodaxe Books

TRANSLATION CHOICE

Juana Iris Goergen • *Sea in My Bones* • the87press
Translated by Silvia R Tandeciarz

PAMPHLET CHOICE

Fahad Al-Amoudi • *When the Flies Come* • ignitionpress

CHOICE SELECTORS RECOMMENDATION SPECIAL COMMENDATION	JO CLEMENT & ROY McFARLANE
TRANSLATION SELECTOR	SHIVANEE RAMLOCHAN
PAMPHLET SELECTORS	NINA MINGYA POWLES & ARJI MANUELPILLAI
CONTRIBUTORS	SOPHIE O'NEILL MEGAN ROBSON LEDBURY CRITICS
EDITORIAL & DESIGN	ALICE KATE MULLEN

Poetry Book Society Memberships

Choice
4 Books a Year: 4 Choice books & 4 *Bulletins* (UK £65, Europe £85, ROW £120)
World
8 Books: 4 Choices, 4 Translation books & 4 *Bulletins* (£98, £160, £190)
Complete
24 Books: 4 Choices, 16 Recommendations, 4 Translations & 4 *Bulletins* (£230, £290, £360)
Single copies of the *Bulletin* £9.99

Cover Artwork by Andropang. Instagram: @andropang
ISBN 9781913129460 ISSN 0551-1690

Poetry Book Society | Milburn House | Dean Street | Newcastle upon Tyne | NE1 1LF
0191 230 8100 | enquiries@poetrybooksociety.co.uk

WWW.POETRYBOOKS.CO.UK

LETTER FROM THE PBS

What a joyous, fascinating, moving and thought-provoking set of selections we have to see you through the Winter. It's a perfect mix of well-established and emerging poets, published by a range of newer, older, large and small publishers. Independent publishing is very close to my heart, so I am really delighted with the rich mix of poets and publishers we are featuring this season.

At Poetry Book Society HQ, as well as selecting the best poetry every season, we are also committed to promoting the work of smaller poetry publishers and lesser-known poets, ensuring that our members and book-buyers have access to as much poetry that is being published and produced in the UK as we can possibly get our hands on. So please do get in touch if there is a poet or publisher you love that is hard to find, and we will do our best to ensure they are available on our website – they might even feature in Meg's Muse e-newsletter!

We'd like to invite you all to listen to our second podcast in partnership with our brilliant pamphlet selector Arji Manuelpillai – a wonderful interview and chat with our Winter Choice poet, Kwame Dawes. If you have a smartphone, you can scan the QR code below or have a listen at www.poetrybooks.co.uk.

This *Bulletin* will reach you all as we approach Christmas and the holiday season, for many a season of giving. Gift vouchers and gift memberships are available from the Poetry Book Society – you can buy online or give us a call and we'll talk you through your options. We think our beautifully packaged Gift Membership is the perfect gift this season, including a special tote bag and free book for your giftee. Also don't forget our gift guide, included in this mailing, is a great resource for some brilliant poetry gift inspiration.

Wishing you all a wonderful end to 2023 and we look forward to seeing what poetry 2024 has to offer. We have a LOT of poetry plans so watch this space!

SOPHIE O'NEILL
PBS & INPRESS DIRECTOR

KWAME DAWES

Kwame Dawes is the author of twenty-six books of poetry and numerous other books of fiction, criticism, and essays. He is Glenna Luschei Editor-in-Chief of *Prairie Schooner* and George W. Holmes University Professor at the University of Nebraska. Dawes is a chancellor of the Academy of American Poets and a fellow of the Royal Society of Literature. His awards include an Emmy, the Felix Dennis Forward Prize for Poetry, a Guggenheim Fellowship, the PEN/Nora Magid Award for Magazine Editing and the Windham Campbell Prize for poetry.

I CHOICE

STURGE TOWN

PEEPAL TREE PRESS | £12.99 | PBS PRICE £9.75

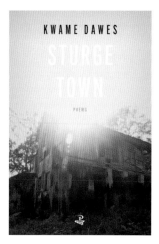

Sturge Town re-encounters the histories and geographies that insist upon Kwame Dawes' imagination. This five-part Pan-Africanist collection convulsively collages the places Ghanaian-born Dawes has lived: Africa, America, Britain and the Caribbean. Consumed with notions of home and the passage of time, wherever and whenever Dawes arrives in a poem, he finds himself "always a foreigner". As in 'Before the Return', he makes sophisticated manoeuvres between personal and collective memory:

> my father's village, thick
> with the scent of rum, where the ghosts
> of slaves inhabit the heavy-leaved
> guinep trees

Alert to the unyielding trajectory of colonialism, this book praises Black dignity and bears especially upon the West Indies' foremost poetries, both in print and in song. St. Lucia's literary giant Derek Walcott's 'The Sea is History' laps euphoniously against the shorelines of Dawes' meticulously considered lyrics. There is deep allusion to Walcott's *The Fortunate Traveller* and 'How I Pray in the Plague' is especially anchored to the title poem's agnostics. Both poets convey the complicated duties of literary art, to serve the poet's fancy and hold a mirror up to society. Embracing "the calming beauty of these puzzles", Dawes will not "offer easy answers" ('Small Talk') and instead writes:

> not as the demander of absolute clarity –
> that would be a crude wickedness –
> but with the fabric of uncertainty
> as a net stretched across the afternoon sky

Sturge Town is one of Jamaica's earliest free villages. There, aged nine, Dawes first heard Bob Marley's working-class rebel reggae lyricism. "The soundtrack of my living", as he writes in *Lyrical Genius*. With their shared motifs of anti-racism, diaspora, gratitude, political protest and romance, *Sturge Town* makes evident that the exiled Trenchtown legend taught Dawes both his Patois and unique mode of revolutionary poetry: words as work, intent on eliciting change in the world.

KWAME DAWES

With *Sturge Town*, I have carved out a body of work that has sought to chronicle the sentiment of my personal histories which are rooted in the histories of my parents and ancestors – it is a history of journey out of Africa and into the world with notable bivouacs in Jamaica, South Carolina and Nebraska; a poetry that relishes the manner in which language can preserve feeling and thought. These poems are intimate and wholly of the moment, even as they are wide-open to the influence of art, music and the literatures that have shaped me. The poem 'It Bruises, Too' finds me on the road encountering another, and finding a reconciliation with that other, who is also myself. There is in this work a meditation on faith, loss, time, and love. I write constantly, and my ritual has been, for the last decade, to write poems in vigorous conversation with art – scattered in my office are art books filled with my poems.

I started to gather these poems after a few years of writing and began to see that my obsessions with faith, time, sightlessness, and the challenges of finding a home in alien places, have galvanised into a theme, a kind of collage of moods and thoughts about journeying. Perhaps I am relieved that poetry lets me capture the feelings of these times, perhaps I am drawn to the way poetry helps me cope with death, with the fear of abandonment, and with the joy of love even while I contend with a world of political disquiet and a persistent reminding of efforts to destroy "my people" over time, and the songs, the hymns, the melodies and art that we have used to resist. So, I put together this book, and found it to be saying everything I want to say right now – in this moment.

> You ask why I wince like that.
> "The silence," I say. "It bruises, too."
> Then, after the elation of this meeting,
> we part, you towards the light, me
> into the gloom you left behind.

KWAME RECOMMENDS

By way of recommendations for poetry reading, there is so much I could say, but what I believe is that the poets who have appeared in the African Poetry Book Fund's *New Generation African Chapbook Boxset* (Akashic Books) – currently nine boxsets of an average of ten new poets in each – constitute an exciting and revelatory introduction to contemporary African poetry. I am deeply moved and challenged by these poets, and strongly recommend that the entire series be read.

MY CHOICE

FEBRUARY LIGHT

The sky offers a brief mellow smile,
a calm pewter assurance, the gentle backdrop
against which the annual death of the sycamore
suggests a priest's instrument of blessing –
the aromatic twigs bundled and dipped in oil
to spray the gathered congregants, or a couple
distracted by the fear of a new beginning,
their awkward bodies learning to consider
coupling. This wash of morning sunlight
will pass quickly enough for us to remark
at the light of our days: "Can you see that?"
"Yes, it is beautiful." This is it: communion
in the grace of the earth's occasional beauty.

WANDERER

How quickly the long-breathed dusks
of summer are wheezing, the light's
softening rapid here in the August end.
The scent of winter, months away,
is already filling the air, and this alien knows
that he's growing familiar with Nebraska.
And yet I don't understand the language
of these long pieces of stripped wood
laid out as a trellis might be, three strips
tied together with the thin bark of local trees,
and then propped up as fragile monuments
of hope or petition, some message
which I do not understand.
But despite my ignorance, I feel a desire
to fall to my knees and make my appeals,
as if such love is given upon request.
How does one say, "Please love me",
so as to be loved fully without question,
despite being unworthy, despite not knowing?
But, I hesitate, stay standing sinfully,
and say, "I am not against your faith,
yet, I continue mine" – which is the immigrant's
protest, as old as strangers arriving in a village,
as old as new believers praying in ancient temples.

BILLY COLLINS

Billy Collins is the author of thirteen books of poetry,
most recently *Whale Day* and *The Rain in Portugal*. He
has received fellowships from the New York Foundation
for the Arts, The National Endowment for the Arts, and
the Guggenheim Foundation. He was chosen by the New
York Public Library to be a "Literary Lion." A graduate
of Holy Cross College, he received his doctorate from
the University of California at Riverside. He is a former
Distinguished Professor of English at Lehman College
(CUNY). He served two terms as United States Poet
Laureate (2001-2003). He is a member of The American
Academy of Arts and Letters.

MUSICAL TABLES

PICADOR | £10.99 | PBS PRICE £8.25

The *New York Times* bestselling poet

BILLY COLLINS

MUSICAL TABLES
POEMS

'Billy Collins puts the 'fun' back in profundity.'
Alice Fulton

There's something mellow and musical about the brevity and slight weight of Collins' *Musical Tables*. These poems explore life from the cradle to the grave. With an astute eye for the world around him, Collins removes the gravity of existence and we encounter a lightness of being.

> I never thought
> of myself
> as a little universe
> inside a big one
> until just now.

This is a poet fascinated by the art of the small poem, as Collins puts it, "they are drastic examples of poetry's way of squeezing large content into tight spaces." Void of the rules of Haiku and Tanka, Collins plays with words in a limited space to see what stumbles out. 'A Small Hotel' alludes to this idea.

> Then a few words
> were seen to stumble out
> in nothing but their nightgown

There are some poems which after you finished reading take you back to the imagined phrase without it ever appearing in the poem, like "the straw that broke the camels back", "hung, drawn and quartered," and "you can hear a pin-drop," this whimsical play on phrases drawn from the margin to make a central poem.

Collins is capturing snapshots of life, often with minute details; the pulse slowed down to the moving shadow of a sundial, the creased eyebrows of a grocer. And when it comes to subjects such as death and illness, like Italo Calvino "when the human realm seems doomed to heaviness, (Collins) feel(s) the need to fly like Perseus into some other space." Whether it's the death of friends in 'The Dead of Winter' or the inevitable ending of life in 'Neighborhood'.

> Before very long.
> I'll be just a breeze
> blowing around town
> trying to avoid all the wind chimes

There's a breeze that blows through this collection, effortlessly turning page after page which makes you fly into some other space.

ROY McFARLANE

SELECTOR'S COMMENT

BILLY COLLINS

Someone in the audience at a reading by Robert Frost had the nerve or the naivety to ask him to explain the poem he had just read. "Oh, you'd like me to say it worse?" came the quick reply. I would say the little poems in *Musical Tables* are good at explaining themselves as quickly as possible. Unlike the more traditional haiku or epigram, the small poem is not an official genre, but it offers a distinct set of pleasures. It knows how to get out of its own way by making a turn almost immediately. The best ones are all turn, pure torque. They're like disappearing acts that vanish with the flip of the page.

Most of mine are untouched by revision; there's no need to meddle with a little group of words that fall into place on the first go. Too short to walk a full pentameter out and back, the small poem keeps its arms around itself. It can sound as natural as a spoken comment, only with a twist. Or think of the small poem as a motion, a pirouette or head-fake. A move or gesture, a gambit without the need for the rest of the game. One of the key attractions of the lyric poem is its brevity. A sonnet can be read in a few minutes, whereas the novelist moves into your house and takes up space on your night table for weeks. The small poem pushes brevity to extremes.

W.S. Merwin has a one-line poem tellingly titled 'Elegy': "Who would I show it to." And Aram Saroyan wins the concision contest with his one-word poem: 'lighght', a neologism that draws attention to the word's silent letters by doubling their soundlessness. Garrulous in comparison, the shortest I could manage here is titled 'Corn Field': "Far from any lake, / I walk in over my head." And just like that, the poem and the poet disappear. Marilyn Monroe, who said she enjoyed reading poetry because it "saves time", would have loved *Musical Tables*. And it would have loved her back.

BILLY RECOMMENDS

Some notable volumes I turn to: Jack Gilbert, *Refusing Heaven* (Knopf); Robert Haas, *Summer Snow* (Ecco); Charles Simic, *Selected Poems 1962-2012* (Faber); Robin Robertson, *Sailing the Forest* (Picador); Greg Delanty, *The Professor of Forgetting* (LSU); Kay Ryan, *The Best of It* (Grove Press); Wisława Szymborska, *Map* (HarperCollins); George Bilgere, *Central Air* (Pitt Poetry Series); Paul Muldoon, *Selected Poems 1968-2016* (Faber); Seamus Heaney, *The Translations* (Faber); Paul Durcan, *Greetings to Our Friends in Brazil* (Harvill); Eamon Grennan, *Out of Sight* (Graywolf Press); Colette Bryce, *Selected Poems* (Picador); Carol Ann Duffy, *The World's Wife* (Picador); Don Paterson, *Selected Poems* (Faber); Nick Laird, *Up Late* (Faber).

RECOMMENDATION

There's so much
going on in the world
besides these sausages

VIEW FROM A BRIDGE

I never thought
of myself
as a little universe
inside a big one
until just now.

JASMINE COORAY

Jasmine Cooray is a poet, psychotherapist and arts facilitator. She has been a Women of the World Festival speaker, BBC Performing Arts Fellow and Writer-in-Residence at the National University of Singapore, and has delivered creative writing projects for The Barbican, the Southbank Centre, First Story, The Arvon Foundation and the National Literacy Trust. Her pamphlet *everything we don't say* was published by Tall Lighthouse in 2009.

INHERITANCE

BAD BETTY PRESS | £10.99 | PBS PRICE £8.25

Jasmine Cooray begins with a journey to the Arctic to scatter her father's ashes and yet he clings to her. "My father with malted Einstein hair / with hair of car-washed skunk." Titles such as 'Now You Are Not Here To Leave Us' and 'Visitor' shows the uneasy juxtaposition of grief and anger, of absence and longing.

The speaker's father's haunting presence allows her or invokes her to bear witness to his journey and know his dreams as in 'Second Generation':

> with a dream of gold streets and electric lights. In the dream,
> their children live freely as kites, though our buoyancy
>
> is terrifying without hands to hold us. Give us the strain
> of the thread, though it hurts, and sometimes cuts the palm.

In her grief Cooray's *Inheritance* becomes a collecting and planting of seeds for a next generation. A call not to forget our ancestors, their ways, traditions, not to forget the racism, the struggles, the hardship. Whether it's "turn(ing) the ingredients of body and garments into a woman" or "...learning to taste the notes that hum through veins" there's a delicious delicacy, in the gathering of her legacy.

Cooray's *Inheritance* is a pot being stirred. By the time we get to the third section, we're introduced to her mother from her Polish side of the family, written like a long poem, broken into six parts:

> of soft skulls and sacrifice, where a tender
> language is spoken, and where my mother,
> her touch soothing and certain and magical,
> is still a cool balm in the fever of our lives.

Inheritance echoes Rilke's instruction "try, like some first human being, to say what you see and experience and love and lose." There's a raw vulnerability, whether spoken for the stage or word-binding for the page, Cooray has exposed herself to the elements of poetry.

ROY McFARLANE

JASMINE COORAY

Inheritance is a collection that speaks to an experience of trying to connect to one's cultural histories when the methods feel complicated and tenuous. It is also a book, in many ways, about loss, and of love poems – to my family, in particular my late father, to my friends, and to my late partner, who died suddenly in 2018. I don't mean love in the idealistic sense – but love that makes room for flaws and disappointments and longing, and love that shows itself upon exiting.

Writing this collection was a way of grounding, of trying to catch the raw, changing and fragmented states of grief, and the love that grief illuminates. In grief, I found myself with a glut of love; desperate to share it, struggling to find "appropriate" places to put it, and at the same time reaching to replicate what was lost. I suppose that's illustrated in poems that describe reaching for intimacy in different ways, each time finding something other than what you hoped for.

This "gap", as I think of it now, also refers to the state one finds oneself in when the trajectory of the life as you imagined did not go to plan. And, if thrown off that trajectory, how do you live? What do you make of your life? There's a great terror, challenge, and creative fertility in that space. Some of the poems, particularly in the last section, I wrote (do I dare to say?) medicinally. I was reading rousing, fiery poems. I needed to make poems that would keep me going, reminders that we don't have to know what to do next, that there will be another future, one which we will find our way through.

> And then there was your laughter
> full of stars, lifting me out of myself
> like someone trapped in a well.

JASMINE RECOMMENDS

Daniel Sluman, *Single Window* (Nine Arches Press); Kim Addonizio, *Wild Nights: New and Selected Poems* (Bloodaxe Books); Richard Scott, *Soho* (Faber); Victoria Adukwei Bulley, *Quiet* (Faber); Roger Robinson, *A Portable Paradise* (Peepal Tree Press).

The world as I knew it had died, bore
a new one, open, open to the sky

WORLD OF WILDFLOWERS

for Will

A packet of wildflower seeds sits
on the mantelpiece, and in it is you.

You would find nature's splashes of colour
on any street, stop to greet the tiniest bloom

as if it were a miniature king, your face lit,
laughter bursting from you like a firework.

This was the richness of how you lived,
and how you live still. Lately we seem

to find flowers in unexpected places:
sunflowers blooming from club speakers,

lavender sprouting between piano keys,
a black cat collared with daisies

and when we, who miss you, embrace,
petals explode between our chests.

Your world was a garden in which to grow
love. You left it open for us to walk in.

JASMINE COORAY

Image: Sophie Davidson

KOSTYA TSOLAKIS

Kostya Tsolakis was born and raised in Athens, Greece, and now lives in London. He is founding editor of *harana poetry*, the online magazine for poets writing in English as a second or parallel language. In 2019 he won the Oxford Brookes International Poetry Competition (ESL category). His poems have been widely published in magazines, including *fourteen poems*, *Magma Poetry*, *Poetry London*, *The Poetry Review* and *Under the Radar*, and anthologies, such as *100 Queer Poems* (Vintage, 2022). His poetry pamphlet *Ephebos* was published by ignitionpress in November 2020. *Greekling* (Nine Arches Press) is his first full collection of poetry.

GREEKLING

NINE ARCHES PRESS | £10.99 | PBS PRICE £8.25

"Greekling" is first recorded in Ben Jonson's *Timber* (1635). The suffix is intended to diminish his subjects. From this coinage, Kostya Tsolakis triumphantly recovers a towering first collection, elegantly buttressed by ekphrases about statues from classical antiquity. With a "hip cocked out sassily", the Motya Charioteer welcomes us into the pleasingly long and musical poem 'marble bf'. Here, Tsolakis brings into language the intricacies of the relic's "no-nonsense / nudity" and decodes its gender-fluid "get-up":

> masc femme Hellenic
> foreign a Greekling
> made like me

Itself a carved monument, 'Someone Else's Child' is a powerful paean to Zak Kostopolous, the anti-fascist HIV activist and drag artist beaten to death by civilians and the officers who should have protected him:

> How they pinned him, handcuffed,
> against the rough, uneven pavement, kicked his heart
> in. A Friday lunchtime in this city.

The speaker, bearing witness, reflects there is "so much police". In '1991' a young speaker privately admires the "semi-divine anatomy" of Perseus and finds more mythic men in museum guidebooks ('Bathroom in an Athens Suburb'). Between clamorous London night buses and dripping neon dance floors, these hearty poems buzz with sexual awakenings. Not all the experiences are consensual, as in the bristling 'Nobody', where we discover that the "hard-to-swallow pill" is rape:

> his body's telling me
> the time to negotiate is over. I discover
> what its like to be a flower pressed
> under a dozen volumes

In the final poem 'On Reading Cavafy During Lockdown' Tsolakis realises he and his childhood muse "write from outside the bounds of Greekness". "How Greek we are in doing so", he reflects. Inviting readers to query our identity and boundaries, as well as those imposed upon us by the state, this sharp collection celebrates and devastates in equal measure.

JO CLEMENT

| SELECTOR'S COMMENT

KOSTYA TSOLAKIS

Greekling is my attempt to reconcile my Greekness with my queerness. Growing up in Athens in the 1990s, I was made to understand that the two were incompatible, that my desiring men was a form of betrayal. In 'freedom or death' I imagine the ghosts of heroes of the Greek War of Independence punishing me for it:

> redseed
> they hiss   their yatagans
> unsheathed

My parents, despite their undeniable love for me, their only child, also made their expectations clear: get married, have children – "those vague-shaped / creatures, still viable in his mind" ('The Light-up Snowman on the Balcony') continue the "line". Despite the loneliness and sense of unbelonging this caused, I resisted the belief that who I am is wrong. Discovering Cavafy at sixteen was a revelation, the first step on my path to converting shame and confusion into self-acceptance, pride and happiness. But to fully achieve this, I had to put a distance between me and my homeland. In England I discovered a less suffocating environment: "not checking myself. What I say, how I look" ('Ghazal: Of Them'). I found a home in London's gay clubs, in Soho's streets. *Greekling* is partly a celebration of the freedoms England offered me, the men I loved, and lost, on the way.

But I couldn't keep my back turned on Greece forever. After I came out to my parents, and fuelled by frustration at the caricaturing of, and lack of empathy with, the people of Greece during the country's financial crisis, I worked on rebuilding my relationship with Greece and my family. This is reflected in the latter half of *Greekling*. So is the fact that reclaiming my place in the society and culture I was born into led to my adding my voice, through poetry, to the Greek LGBTQ+ community's fight for visibility – our protest against the injustices and violence committed towards queer people, women, and all those perceived not to fit the Greek "mould", not to mention our maltreated natural environment.

KOSTYA RECOMMENDS

Adelaide Ivánova, *the hammer and other poems* (Poetry Translation Centre); Eduardo C. Corral, *Guillotine* (Graywolf); Emma Jeremy, *sad thing angry* (Out-Spoken Press); Fiona Moore, *The Distal Point* (HappenStance); Heidi Williamson, *Return by Minor Road* (Bloodaxe); Iulia David, *Blueprint* (Green Bottle Press); Jennifer Wong, *Letters Home* (Nine Arches Press); Leo Boix, *Ballad of a Happy Immigrant* (Chatto); Mícheál McCann, *Keeper* (fourteen poems); Romalyn Ante, *Antiemetic for Homesickness* (Chatto); Paul Stephenson, *Hard Drive* (Carcanet); Sean Wai Keung, *sikfan glaschu* (Verve Poetry); Victoria Adukwei Bulley, *Quiet* (Faber).

I recognise you
for the curious   unbelonging
thing you truly are
masc   femme   Hellenic
foreign   a Greekling
made like me

ON REREADING CAVAFY DURING LOCKDOWN

There you are, namesake, tracer
of half-remembered pleasure.

I read your words until darkness
covers them, see your shadow
in the corner: a hunched figure,
unguarded eyes behind round spectacles.

I too have put down words that defy
those who wish to retouch my desire. I too
write from outside the bounds of Greekness;
yet how Greek we are in doing so.

Each time I read your words,
you offer my lips, with a steady hand,
a tall, cold glass of water –
to wash the fruit down.

KOSTYA TSOLAKIS

DAVID WHEATLEY

David Wheatley was born in Dublin in 1970. He is the author of five previous collections of poetry, including *The President of Planet Earth* (Carcanet, 2017), *Thirst* (Galley Press, 1997) which won the Rooney Prize for Irish Literature; *Misery Hill* (2000); *Mocker* (2006) and *A Nest on the Waves* (2010) and a novel *Stretto* (CB Editions, 2022). He has also coedited with Ailbhe Darcy *The Cambridge History of Irish Women's Poetry* (Cambridge University Press, 2021). He lives in rural Aberdeenshire.

CHILD BALLAD

CARCANET PRESS | £12.99 | PBS PRICE £9.75

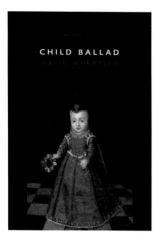

Woven with Scots dialect, David Wheatley's *Child Ballad* adopts its title from the narrative folk songs anthologised by Francis Child in the nineteenth century. Drawn from local history and legend, *The English and Scottish Popular Ballads* often feature families entangled in loyalties and circumstances of the heart. Wheatley's lyrics sometimes share the ballad's aloof omniscience and allude to variations of these dramatic old yarns. Through the lens of fatherhood, he also navigates contemporary concerns, as in the witty 'Long Slide', in which subcultures collide:

> I am galumphing round the soft-play centre
> like something from Brueghel...
> all food-stained flapping jumper and odd socks

In 'Child Ballad' a devoted poet-father's anxieties are conferred upon savvy "freeborn" daughter Morven, who asks "What songs you sing me... will I still know and sing long decades hence?". Other poems speak with the bawdiness of 'Kempy Kay' (Ballad 33) such as 'A Clashindarroch Wildcat for Tom Pickard'. The Aberdeenshire animal speaks through "teeth smeared / with gralloch" as it asks of its own – and perhaps humanity's – endangerment:

> how do you want
>   my extinction event
> picturesque or
>   with blood on the snow

An Irish poet living in Scotland, Wheatley's poems cleave to and from these territories and landscapes, their languages, and literary traditions. As we discover in 'Portrait of a Man Thought to Be Andrew Marvell', post-Brexit Britain is an uncertain place where we can "feel the ground shift". The collection lands on steadier foundations in the long eco-poem 'A Curious Herbal'. Here, a family bonds through citizen science, following roaming badgers and sporing "next year's puff- / balls" with gentle kicks. Wheatley generously invites his readers to share a moment in the optimistic glee of a "two-year- / old botanist" who:

> rolls in the leaves
>   announces
> 'we can be
>   mushrooms too'

JO CLEMENT

DAVID WHEATLEY

Among the most celebrated of modern Irish poems is Derek Mahon's 'A Disused Shed in Co. Wexford', in which a mushroom colony trapped in darkness for decades yearns for release into the light. It makes for beguiling political allegory, but less convincing mycology; darkness and damp are ideal conditions for fungi. The poetical history of mushrooms, it must be said, has not always been a happy one. The Romantics did not care for them and Emily Dickinson, aware of their lowly status, wrote "Had Nature an Apostate / That Mushroom – it is Him!"

More recently Ailbhe Darcy has suggested "Mushrooms could grow on a person all the same". Standing inside a dark pinewood in rural Aberdeenshire contemplating the first fly agarics of the year with my mushroom-besotted daughter, I am inclined to agree. While the appearance of these spotted red caps above ground is always cause for celebration, we are aware that they are only the visible tip of an underground network, or mycelium – a thread-like nervous system extending over huge swathes of the wood below our feet. Should one part of the wood catch fire, the whole forest will twitch with the news. So despite Mahon's protestations, the mushrooms may not have been as cut off from the wider world as his poem suggests.

My book *Child Ballad* ends with a long poem about my daughter and her mycophilia, in which I harvest the lore we have acquired on our woodland walks. The woods are cold and damp. Sunlight is scarce, but I do not yearn for the brighter days of summer. I tread on a puffball mushroom and it emits its copious spore-cloud. The much-blackened page of the mycelium braces to receive our latest impressions. "Even now", to return to that Mahon poem, "there are places where a thought might grow."

DAVID RECOMMENDS

George Oppen, *Of Being Numerous* (New Directions); Lorine Niedecker, *North Central* (Fulcrum Press); Edited by Angus Macleod, *Songs of Duncan Ban MacIntyre* (Scottish Gaelic Texts Society); Arthur Johnston, *Musa Latina Aberdonensis* (New Spalding Club); *Thomas Percy's Reliques of Ancient English Poetry* (Everyman); Pierre Reverdy, *La lucarne ovale* (Birault); Ailbhe Darcy, *Imaginary Menagerie* (Bloodaxe Books).

RECOMMENDATION

I am citizen, not subject, freeborn
daughter of the future I will earn

CHILD BALLAD (EXTRACT)

I Morven Aifric Sadhbh, a child of winter,
doomed to follow where my parents wander,
came unstuck swapping the womb's dark amber
for the paltry welcomes of November.

Mother, father, brother offered comfort
after all that way I'd come for it.
Out of the granite city I was carried
to where that shining silver stone is quarried,

and past the silent playground where I'll test
the reach and grip of infant foot and fist.
My first assertive cries dispersed across
the damp fields mobbed by surly flights of crows.

Dear family, I see that we're alike
if not the same. Whatever I might lack
I claim as mine with busy, grasping hands untrained for
now in telling foes from friends,

but glad to find a yielding breast in reach.
For all your pressing kindnesses I pledge
a stored-up gratitude you may decode
from teenage eyebrows raised and blank eyes rolled.

Whose life grows, whose wilts and falls away?
What waiting futures do my two palms weigh?
What songs you sing me round our daily haunts
will I still know and sing long decades hence?

I see our house is ballasted with junk,
where books accumulate and bookshelves sink.
What trace, tell me, should I hope to add
to all that you have thought and dreamt and said?

DAVID WHEATLEY

MARJORIE LOTFI

Marjorie Lotfi was born in New Orleans, moved to Tehran as a baby with her American mother and Persian father, and fled Iran with one suitcase and an hour's notice during the Iranian Revolution. She lived in different parts of the US before moving to the UK in 1999 and to Scotland in 2005. Her pamphlet *Refuge*, poems about her childhood in revolutionary Iran, was published by Tapsalteerie Press in 2018. She was awarded the inaugural James Berry Poetry Prize in 2021. She has been the Poet in Residence at Jupiter Artland, Spring Fling and the Wigtown Book Festival, and was commissioned to write *Pilgrim*, a sequence about migration between Iran and the US, for the St Magnus Festival on Orkney. She founded the Belonging Project involving over 1500 refugees across Scotland, and is a co-founder and Director of the charity Open Book. She is an Ignite Fellow with the Scottish Book Trust, one of the 12 Collective of women writers, co-editor of New Writing Scotland, and chair of the board of StAnza, Scotland's International Poetry Festival.

SPECIAL COMMENDATION

THE WRONG PERSON TO ASK

BLOODAXE BOOKS | £10.99 | PBS PRICE £8.25

The Wrong Person to Ask is to "colour, a breath of wind, the perfection of shadows," to borrow from Lotfi's opening epigraph by John Burnside. This collection has the breath of wind fluttering though its pages, subtle and imbuing. Lotfi shares the young refugee experience by folding innocence into the nightmare of conflict like a"body folded into the namaz", Shah's guards and teenager skateboarding, hiding mother and father as if it was a game, and "crossing the street for mother's cigarettes".

Interwoven are ekphrastic poems, news headlines and references to movies, shining light on the misery and failings, the scars and terrors of exile and migrant crossing. Like sonnets, a witness to "others" with a volta towards her own lived experience, the pain and personal journey as in 'Gabriella's Dream' or 'What You See in the Dark':

> you there, hijabed and waiting for language
> you there, foreigner, brown as the soil
> you there, a keeper of words
> you there, a stranger to yourself, awake in the night

Where the first section asks questions of flight, of being uprooted, the second section asks what it's like to finally find roots, what is home? Is it at The Luing Sound and Fladda Lighthouse, fishing for the common lobster or the Scottish rain that keeps on coming. This collection is light as the haar coming in from the sea, filled with wonder and stramash as in 'After the Match':

> But the dark is not the dark
> to the blind, only more
> of the same, the way
> the dead boy is never
> dead to his mother.

Loss echoes through this collection; loved ones, the voices of the many lost at sea trying to find a safe haven, or national (collective) moments of grief. Home is a sense of absence as well as being present but Lotfi leaves a light ablaze, "like a candle in a cathedral, for the keeping of vigil".

ROY McFARLANE

ON SEEING IRAN IN THE NEWS, I WANT TO SAY

my grandmother was called Nasreen,
that she died two years ago in Tabriz
and I couldn't go to say goodbye,
that she knew nothing of power,
nuclear or otherwise. I want to say
that the bonfires for *Chahar Shanbeh Suri*
were built by our neighbour's hands;
as children we were taught to jump over
and not be caught by the flames. I want to say
my cousin Elnaz, the one born after I left,
has a son and two degrees in Chemistry,
and had trouble getting a job. I want to say
that the night we swam towards
the moon hanging over the horizon
of the Caspian Sea, we found ourselves
kneeling on a sandbar we couldn't see
like a last gift. I want to say
I'm the wrong person to ask.

JUANA IRIS GOERGEN

SILVIA R. TANDECIARZ

Juana Iris Goergen (Puerto Rico) is a poet and Emerita Professor at DePaul University, Chicago and Visiting Professor at InterAmerican University, Arecibo, Puerto Rico. She has published four poetry collections and edited nine anthologies. Juana launched and co-organised the Chicago International Poetry Festival Poesía en Abril for eleven years. She was awarded Contratiempo Poesía/Cultura Award in 2014 and the José Revueltas Poetry Award in 2018. In 2019 she was honoured by the International Poetry Festival Poesía en Abril Committee and DePaul University with a poetry award that bears her name, the Juana Iris Goergen Poetry Award.

Silvia R. Tandeciarz is Chancellor Professor of Modern Languages and Literatures and Vice Dean for Social Sciences and Interdisciplinary Studies at William & Mary. A translator, poet and scholar, she has published widely in the field of Latin American Cultural Studies, including *Citizens of Memory: Affect, Representation, and Human Rights in Postdictatorship Argentina* (2017, Bucknell University Press) which appeared in Spanish in 2020 and the poetry collection *Exorcismos* (Betania, 2000).

TRANSLATION CHOICE

SEA IN MY BONES: MAR EN LOS HUESOS
BY JUANA IRIS GOERGEN, TRANS. SILVIA R. TANDECIARZ

THE87PRESS | £14.99 | PBS PRICE £11.25

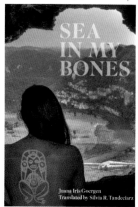

When fleeing from the ghosts of our trauma, from what source do we derive our salvation? In Juana Iris Goergen's fourth collection of poetry, *Sea in my Bones* (*Mar en los Huesos*), the answer might seem evident, almost immediate: find yourself in ancestral waters. Yet the journey inscribed by the poet, in this four-part circumnavigation through the navel of an exploitative history, is a cyclical immersion, not a launchpad dive.

Guiding her reader through extractive archives of conquest and depredation in the Caribbean, Goergen summons a trinity of tongues that do not ask the English language for permission: Taíno, Yoruba, and Spanish. In Taíno origin stories, the speaker of the poems shapes the Caribbean archipelago as it was before foreign incursion, calling on an undisputable richness of Arawakan mythology to orient the world itself. Summoning Yoruba deities and ceremonies of faith, the poet further populates the landscape conjured by her speaker, establishing dynasties of rule, pillars of resistance held onto by Black communities subject to unspeakable atrocities.

The Spanish that weaves and wends not one, but a convergence of, pathways – you might enthusiastically call them spirit ways, and not be incorrect – is compulsive in its generosity, lavish in its descriptions. One senses a matched expansiveness in Silvia R. Tandeciarz's English translation, which never simplifies or flattens Goergen's effusions of ritual, lore, and polyvocal survival. The worlds, plural, of these poems are apposite forces to denial: they stare long at the transatlantic slave trade; the colonial suppression of African people's ways of enduring slavery; the refusals against such erasure that rooted themselves in song, food, dance, and Santería.

A love song of defiance, a paean of Puerto Rican ferocity and Caribbean autonomous joy, *Sea in my Bones* is a consummate exploration of the soul, refracted through every age of trauma and tenacity that can be told.

> never ending
> never ending
> never ending.

SHIVANEE RAMLOCHAN

XII

Batú ciba batey/ The ball hard as stone is in the batey.

2.

Without hands[1]
you will be more blue
more water
more beginning.

Vibrating conjunction. Exact in equanimity.

The sea
will carry your name in its foam.
The multitude of living and dead
will turn with precision to the reason of your beginning.

In the Batú,
you rise from the depths of your being.
You transcend the event's mere occurrence.
Atebeane nequen,—the honorable women,
buried with their caciques—They know it.

In the Batú
All is you
you, are All.
The Toa—great river— looks like you.
Image and likeness.

TRANSLATED BY SILVIA R. TANDECIARZ

Batú is a ball game played without using your hands

FAHAD AL-AMOUDI

Fahad Al-Amoudi is a writer and editor of Ethiopian and Yemeni heritage based in London. His work is published in *The Poetry Review, Wasafiri, The London Magazine, Mizna* and *Butcher's Do*g. He was the winner of *The White Review* Poet's Prize 2022 and was shortlisted for the Brunel International African Poets Prize 2022 and Pat Kavanagh Prize 2023. Fahad is a graduate of the Writing Squad, member of Malika's Poetry Kitchen, Reviews Editor for *Magma* and an Editorial Assistant at *OWN IT!*

WHEN THE FLIES COME

IGNITION   PRESS | £6.00 |

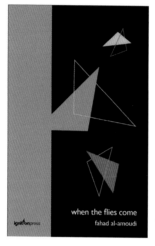

when the flies come
fahad al-amoudi

ignitionpress

The opening poem of *When the Flies Come* hooked me and did not leave me for days. In "i. Cicada" the atmosphere is alive and redolent. There's movement in the air, a kind of electric charge borne out of leaving and longing. A tidal pull towards somewhere else. Elemental and geological imagery propel these moments where memories break through the poem's surface:

This island is one grain of rock salt slowly dissolving in the water. Ayat, everything is bitter.

This current of energy is felt through many of Al-Amoudi's poems, but especially the sequence of biographical poems that take the form of imagined letters written by Prince Alemayehu, who was taken to England from Ethiopia in 1868 against his mother's will. Al-Amoudi shows his immense skill as a poet of history and biography, conjuring a voice that is both contemporary and of another era. The prose poem lends itself particularly well to working in a sequence. They echo each other, and within each we feel the blur of displacement:

Fields of peonies become roses become lilies

'Bedtime' marks an interesting shift in the pamphlet's rhythm, a fluid and surreal ode to a city at night. There's a dreamlike strangeness here that compels you to revisit the poem a second and third time, to dwell in this restless world a little longer, where lots of instantaneous transformations take place. In other poems, a vending machine becomes a luminous shrine; a prayer rug becomes a slice of sky.

When the Flies Come is an accomplished, prismatic study of boyhood and grief, taking countless bold imaginative leaps. 'V. in the time it takes to pose for a photo a country disappears' is another staggering prose poem:

if the page is an abyss words are the peaks that stare into the gorge. i am a vulture unpicking language down to the marrow.

SELECTOR'S COMMENT

ARJI MANUELPILLAI & NINA MINGYA POWLES

III. UNSENT (CIRCA. 1878)

We met in the spring, the world opened
like a pistachio. You were everything I wasn't
expecting to find – a wish at the end
of a dandelion seed. You said I was a library,
quiet and sun-spotted, a leopard
sleeping in a tree.

That was the year I read Byron and Shelley,
not much else. It's easy to mistake longing
for love, that parasol affair. My shadow
is irredentist. I stay by the creek, the water
imperceptibly deep. This, I tell myself,
is easy – a spectator to my own desire.

With you, I speak with closed lips
for fear I might swallow a flood.

WINTER BOOK REVIEWS

OLGA DERMOTT-BOND: FRIEZE
REVIEWED BY SHASH TREVETT

A debut of inventive poems which skilfully mine art, myth, religion and literature to present the familiar in new and quietly satisfying ways. Dermott-Bond has the knack of looking around corners to write about things and people who inhabit the slightly-off-stage: Aunt Em from *The Wizard of Oz*, Blanche Ingram from *Jane Eyre*, the clasp on the dress of Millais's Ophelia. Whether writing about the death of a father, or a miscarriage, this is a poet skilled at inhabiting the skin of other people's lives.

OCTOBER | NINE ARCHES PRESS | £10.99 | PBS PRICE £8.25

CHRIS EMERY: MODERN FOG
REVIEWED BY ANNIE FAN

The best poems in this collection have a "provincial wool purpose", a fogginess to their landscape of "humans and birds" and lost religions that makes the faraway familiar. The city poems are clearer and less inviting: canals of condoms and "slave-financed squares" overspill with characters and colours that don't quite juxtapose but distract from Emery's otherwise tight, talented grasp on nature – human nature.

NOVEMBER | ARC | £10.99 | PBS PRICE £8.25

KATHRYN GRAY: HOLLYWOOD OR HOME
REVIEWED BY OLUWASEUN S. OLAYIWOLA

"The mind is a terrible cabinet, / populated by indescribable figurines." Hollywood is one cabinet, with figurines of lost, abused actors, greedy moguls, and demagogic politicians. But the mind of the solitary poet, too, flails at its own evanescence: "I want to be a star. I'd die for my art. But I worry no one would care." *Hollywood Or Home*, its hymnal under-thrumming, demonstrates how Hollywood's eminence disfigures success. Gray's own "sack of regrets" fashions a wondrous meditation on the vicissitudes of a life spent in art-making.

Hollywood or Home
Kathryn Gray

OCTOBER | SEREN | £9.99 | PBS PRICE £7.50

LEDBURY CRITICS TAKEOVER

Kearns' fallen things are set out visually (moths, superheroes, parachutes, coffins) and tonally: "you start every new day with gunfire as salutation." When not engaging in "botched attempts" at inventory-ing, this book-length poem tries to fell what cannot fall: the mystery of death, "the dark corner of not knowing"; that which is "inevitable" but by no means "simple". *On The Subject of Fallen Things* weaves a philosophical tapestry of "exit(s)... contained in the entrance."

NOVEMBER | BAD BETTY PRESS | £10.99 | PBS PRICE £8.25

"Form / is always the answer to the riddle it poses," one speaker says in this radiantly engrossing collection. Lerner's poems, with a hypnotising sonic urgency, untangle the guiding "lights" of family, faith, creation, and language itself. From the outset, Lerner poignantly thematises the crumbling line between poetry and prose, as in 'Index of Themes': "Poems about you, prose / poems." These poems are stars in the night of meaning, preferring to be sensed by their seductive glow, their emanation. *The Lights* is a masterwork.

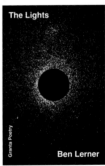

OCTOBER | GRANTA | £12.99 | PBS PRICE £9.75

Kent's second collection, his first with radical publishing collective the87press, is in part a satire of the book's projected reception among Britain's conservative and classist literary institutions. *The Working Classic* alternates between short sequences of lyrics from imaginary pamphlets – comically dubbed Kent's "debut" – and long prosaic interludes. The book has fun with its premise, and its critique is sharp, but at times the satire can overwhelm the poems' more nuanced touches.

OCTOBER | THE87PRESS | £14.99 | PBS PRICE £11.75

BOOK REVIEWS

ABIGAIL PARRY: I THINK WE'RE ALONE NOW
REVIEWED BY SHASH TREVETT

A collection which looks through, around and beyond words, dissecting their "hinges and joints" in poems which are playfully skilful and intellectually rigorous in equal measure. Parry ranges across centuries and disciplines (Latin and Middle English nestle companionably next to the scientific and the popular) so that Wittgenstein finds a partner with Radiohead and Humphrey Bogart with Chrétien de Troyes. This is a collection dripping with the "flair / for the theatre", with words taking centre stage: a love song to language itself.

NOVEMBER | BLOODAXE | £12.00 | PBS PRICE £9.00

ED. POTTS & PESTANO: MENOPAUSE ANTHOLOGY
REVIEWED BY SHASH TREVETT

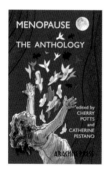

A timely anthology both celebrating and lamenting a woman's womb "tick(ing) its last tock" (Cath Holland). Spanning poems and tightly constructed micro-fictions, this anthology is primordial, featuring women who are warriors, who have spent decades fighting or celebrating their bodies until now, eulogising their last eggs, they choose to release the "shamanic" power (Alyson Hallett) of the menopause on those around them. Beautifully curated, this anthology is a lovely mixture of measured thought and explosive humour.

OCTOBER | ARACHNE PRESS | £9.99 | PBS PRICE £7.50

SENI SENEVIRATNE: THE GO-AWAY BIRD
REVIEWED BY DAVE COATES

A collection of occasional lyrics, ekphrastic sequences, love poems and travelogues, the imaginative horizons of Seneviratne's fourth book are admirably broad. Seneviratne has a great facility for imaginative empathy, and the book's centrepiece, 'Naming the Pages', ventriloquising unnamed child slaves featured in 17th and 18th century aristocratic portraits, is well-researched and passionately achieved. While some postcard poems fall a little flat, pieces like 'Night Calls' and 'Red' have a fabulous intensity, cut close to the bone.

OCTOBER | PEEPAL TREE PRESS | £9.99 | PBS PRICE £7.50

Any retrospective risks indulgence, but *Hell I Love Everybody: 52 Poems* by James Tate retains his piercing sense of humour and unflinching gaze; not lyric, not quite joke, but something in between that sits at the intersection of performance and page. Tate's speakers are invisible characters, peripheral to society, but find humour or heartbreak or both in these lines – and any reader would do the same.

OCTOBER | CARCANET | £14.99 | PBS PRICE £11.25

PETER WALLIS: HALF OTHER
REVIEWED BY OLUWASEUN S. OLAYIWOLA

This debut begins in the interstitial space between twin boys' births, the time it takes to "boil two eggs consecutively." Wallis's twins are "symmetrical", "answers to a multiple-choice question". Formally and at times stirringly, they have simile-brain: scenes recount one twin standing over the other at a crucial medical scan, a symbolic wallet passed from one to the other, like "an Aztec Offering." Illness individualises and *Half Other* makes a paradox of this in twin brotherhood.

OCT | HIPPOCRATES PRESS | £10.00 | PBS PRICE £7.50

ED. McCARTHY WOOLF & TEITLER: MAPPING THE FUTURE
REVIEWED BY OLUWASEUN S. OLAYIWOLA

A landmark text in British poetry, *Mapping the Future* reunites the thirty fellows of The Complete Works – a who's who of contemporary British poetry – with selections of new poetic and critical writing. Where the original anthologies foregrounded novelty, here are those same artists in full artistic maturity, with conviction and force behind their ambitions, curiosities, solidarities and visions. Bernadine Evaristo's introduction ends with a warning, however: "Doors that we have prised open can just as quickly be shut on us".

OCTOBER | BLOODAXE | £14.99 | PBS PRICE £11.25

BOOK REVIEWS

WINTER PAMPHLETS

— TAHER ADEL: I DON'T KNOW WHAT LANGUAGE I DREAM IN —

From the opening titular poem, British-Bahraini poet Taher Adel's pamphlet is full of shots to the heart, striking the reader with emotional episodes and hard truths, in language which is stunningly wrought even as the poet wrestles with his relationship with that language. The reader is made very aware of this – there is an inescapable feeling of the struggle of having to translate the hardships that Adel describes. An impactful and valuable work.

BURNING   EYE   BOOKS | £6.99 |

KYM DEYN: DIONYSIA

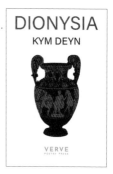

A colourful cast of dramatis personae from a Fortune Teller to Thessalonike, "Myth-sister" of Alexander the Great, join this dionysian jaunt through Ancient Greece. Deyn's playful polyphony of voices skilfully rewrites the classics, reminding us of the slippery nature of history, "the story is a wild geranium", and the malleability of mythology. Tarot and epic storytelling combine in *Dionysia* to oracular effect: "I'm Homer if you believe me, and Cassandra if you don't".

VERVE   PRESS | £7.99 |

SARAH DOYLE: (M)OTHERSONGS

Sarah Doyle's striking pamphlet explores deeply personal experiences of non-motherhood, endometriosis, infertility and "the faces of children / you will not have". These are poignant and painful poems, "twisted into promise", which will resonate with all those who are coming to terms with childlessness. Despite "the othering nature of un-motherhood", as Polly Atkins so eloquently puts it, *(M)othersongs* bravely sings of "belief, courage, hope."

V.   PRESS | £6.50 |

LABONI ISLAM: TRIMMING THE WICK

Flowing between Bangladesh and Toronto, each poem is poised like "a vowel / between two continents". Laboni Islam inherits and inhabits the climate catastrophe of her ancestral Bangladesh, mapping a life lived precariously, like a flood plain: "I would say my love is a complicated country, barely above sea level." Yet this debut is not just "flooding but breathing". *Trimming the Wick* shows us how to carefully light a hurricane lantern "like courage" and how to "hold... history like a hurricane" – lit and utterly living.

IGNITION   PRESS | £6.00 |

JACK COOPER: BREAK THE NOSE OF EVERY BEAUTIFUL THING

Poetry and Science meet in the practice of close observation in this Eric Gregory Award-winning pamphlet. Trained in biomedical research, Cooper treats us to thrilling poetry describing scientific subjects and procedures, and then turns his sharp eye and enchanting language to romantic, sexual, and familial relationships. Love, art, life: there is much waiting to be discovered in this illuminating work.

DOOMSDAY   PRESS | £8.00 |

TWENTY-ONE POEMS ABOUT WONKY ANIMALS

The Wonky Animals Poetry Collective are joined by names new and familiar in this engaging mini-anthology. Inhabiting a spectrum of animality and humanity, the poems look at the animal in us, and consider how animals inform our emotional lives, how we can learn from them as people and as poets. This is a celebration of the wonky, and an uplifting and comforting read for when we're feeling a little wonky ourselves.

CANDLESTICK   PRESS | £6.99 |

Celeste Augé	I Imagine Myself	Salmon Publishing	£11.00
Bob Beagrie	Eftwyrd	Smokestack Books	£8.99
Ilaria Boffa	Beginnings & Other Tragedies	Valley Press	£12.99
Olga Dermott-Bond	Frieze	Nine Arches Press	£10.99
Ed. Edna Bonhomme	After Sex	Silver Press	£13.99
Kate Bolton Bonnici	A True & Just Record	Boiler House Press	£12.99
C D Boyland	Mephistopheles	Blue Diode Press	£10.00
Matthew Caley	To Abandon Wizardry	Bloodaxe Books	£12.00
Cambell & Henderson	Small Plates	Broken Sleep Books	£11.99
Seamus Cashman	Talking Down the Clocks	Salmon Publishing	£11.00
Ed. Jess Chandler	Seven Rooms	Prototype Publishing	£15.00
Sabeen Chaudhry	Rimming the Event Horizon	the87press	£14.99
Nebin K Chhetri	I, Father	Black Spring Press Group	£11.99
Billy Collins	Musical Tables	Picador	£10.99
Jasmine Cooray	Inheritance	Bad Betty Press	£10.99
Mike Corrao	The Persimmon is an Event	Broken Sleep Books	£12.99
Rachel Coventry	The Detachable Heart	Salmon Publishing	£11.00
Andrea Davidson	Eggenwise	The Emma Press	£5.99
Gram Joel Davies	Not Enough Rage	V. Press	£10.99
Kwame Dawes	Sturge Town	Peepal Tree Press	£12.95
Gary Day	The Glass Roof Falls as Rain	Holland Park Press	£10.00
John F. Deane	Selected and New Poems	Carcanet Press	£16.99
Theo Dorgan	Once Was A Boy	Dedalus Press	£11.00
Chris Emery	Modern Fog	Arc Publications	£10.99
Kayla Martell Feldman	Same Story	Verve Poetry Press	£10.99
Jasmine Games	Somebody's Daughter	Black Spring Press Group	£11.99
Dani Gill	Lessons in Kindness	Salmon Publishing	£11.00
Kathryn Gray	Hollywood or Home	Seren	£9.99
Jess Green	Dressed as Love	Burning Eye Books	£9.99
Fee Griffin	Really Not Really	Broken Sleep Books	£11.99
John Griffin	Erosions	Salmon Publishing	£11.00
David Grundy	A True Account	the87press	£14.99
Philip Hancock	House on the A34	CB editions	£10.00
Kaycee Hill	Hot Sauce	Bloodaxe Books	£10.99
Lynne Hjelmgaard	The Turpentine Tree	Seren	£9.99
Ciarán Hodgers	Solastalgia	Burning Eye Books	£9.99
Nicholas Hogg	Missing Person	Broken Sleep Books	£9.99
Kit Ingram	Aqueous Red	Broken Sleep Books	£11.99
Anita Kaminska	Power Less Mess	Arc Publications	£10.99
Alicia Byrne Keane	Pretend Cartoon Strength	Broken Sleep Books	£11.99
James Kearns	On the Subject of Fallen Things	Bad Betty Press	£10.99
Aaron Kent	The Working Classic	the87press	£14.99
Jade King	Sucker Punch	Broken Sleep Books	£10.99
Daniel Kramb	Little Estuaries	HetMoet-Menard Press	£10.99
John Robert Lee	Belmont Portfolio	Peepal Tree Press	£9.99
Angela Leighton	Something, I Forget	Carcanet Press	£12.99
Ben Lerner	The Lights	Granta Poetry	£12.99
Fran Lock	Vulgar Errors / Feral Subjects	Out-Spoken Press	£12.99
Marjorie Lotfi	The Wrong Person to Ask	Bloodaxe Books	£10.99
MacGillivray	Ravage	Bloodaxe Books	£14.99
A.V. Marraccini	We The Parasites	Boiler House Press	£12.99
Shane McCrae	The Many Hundreds of the Scent	Corsair	£12.99
Katherine Meehan	Dame Julie Andrews' Botched Vocal...	Two Rivers Press	£10.99